HER HUSBA

J

A Wife's Ministry and a Minister's Wife

Sara J. Leone

An excellent wife is the crown
of her husband (*Prov.* 12:4).

THE BANNER OF TRUTH TRUST

THE BANNER OF TRUTH TRUST
3 Murrayfield Road, Edinburgh EH12 6EL, UK
PO Box 621, Carlisle, PA 17013, USA

*

© Banner of Truth 2007

ISBN-10: 0 85151 946 6
ISBN-13: 978 0 85151 946 3

*

Typeset in 10/12.5 pt Adobe Caslon
at the Banner of Truth Trust

Printed in the USA by
VersaPress, Inc.,
East Peoria, IL

INTRODUCTION

In the fall of 2005, the wives of students at Reformed Presbyterian Theological Seminary, Pittsburgh, where my husband, Scott, was studying, met to consider the topic 'The Responsibilities of a Pastor's Wife'. Due to other commitments, I was not able to travel to this gathering, but I did manage to contribute to the discussion *in absentia* by sending in a list of responsibilities as I understood them. Some time later, my husband suggested that I should think about writing further on this subject, using the list I had drawn up as a possible outline. Without his suggestion, I would not have written this booklet. Thank you, Scott, for your advice and constant support. I would also like to thank Ann O'Neill for her kindness in encouraging me to complete this little project.

In his grace the Lord has provided me with many positive examples of Christian wives, including my mother and sisters. I also wish to thank Anita, Anne, Bev, Cathi, Gail, Ginny, Iamma, Joie, Mairi, Margaret, Sally, and Susanne for the way each of you have exemplified cheerful, loving support for your husbands in their work as ministers of Christ's gospel.

Some time ago, I read several books and articles about the call to the ministry and the qualifications necessary for ministers. However I found it well-nigh impossible to find much to read on the related subject of the life of a pastor's wife. A balance needs to be maintained between, on the one hand, elevating the pastor's wife to the position of 'The First Lady of the Church', and on the other, brushing off any particular obligations on her part by claiming that she is just another member of the church. All pastors' wives have certain basic responsibilities laid upon them. My prayer is that this booklet will encourage and help pastors' wives in their practical service for the Lord.

While I have written primarily for those who are the wives of pastors, I hope that this booklet will be a blessing to many Christian women in the fulfilling of their own special responsibilities. May you be encouraged to pray for and support your own pastor and his wife.

> Jesus, Master, whom I serve,
> Though so feebly and so ill,
> Strengthen hand and heart and nerve
> All Thy bidding to fulfil.
> Open Thou mine eyes to see
> All the work Thou hast for me.
>
> Lord, Thou needest not, I know,
> Service such as I can bring;
> Yet I long to prove and show
> Full allegiance to my King.
> Thou an honour art to me;
> Let me be a praise to Thee.
>
> *Frances Ridley Havergal*

SARA J. LEONE
Carlisle, Pa.,
Fall 2006.

I

PROVIDE A QUIET, PEACEFUL HOME FOR YOUR HUSBAND

Your wife shall be like a fruitful vine in the very heart of your house (Psa. 128:3).

When thinking about marriage, we need to consider its origin and purpose. According to the Scriptures, God formed the first man and, after declaring all created things to be very good, stated that it was *not* good that he was alone (*Gen.* 1:31; 2:18). It was our gracious God who saw the need and provided what was lacking in Adam's life. God made a woman and brought her to the man to be his companion and wife. Eve's purpose was to complete Adam; she was to be his 'help-meet' or 'suitable-helper'.

Today, wives have the high privilege of being true companions to their husbands, supplying what they need. When asked to describe a minister's wife, Dr Martyn Lloyd-Jones included in his response the following comments: 'Her main business is to look after her husband – relieve him of worries about the home, about food, as far as she can about financial matters . . . She is to protect him and to help him.'[1] In this chapter we will explore our responsibility for providing a place of refuge for our husbands in the ministry.

What kind of day did your husband experience in the work of the ministry? Perhaps he visited the sick, the dying, or the spiritually careless. As a pastor he has the care of the sheep weighing heavily on his mind. We read of this in 2 Corinthians 11:28. After listing the dreadful persecutions and hardships he had endured, the apostle Paul spoke of one more burden he bore, '. . . what comes upon me daily: my deep concern for all the churches.' Your husband may have

---

[1] Quoted in Iain H. Murray, *D. Martyn Lloyd-Jones: The Fight of Faith*, (Edinburgh: Banner of Truth, 1990), p. 762.

encountered unexpected opposition from church members, or from fellow ministers in his denomination. Perhaps an urgent telephone call from the hospital intruded on his time set aside for sermon preparation. Quite possibly he may have just received notice that the aging family vehicle is in need of repairs that will put a serious hole in the family budget. Furthermore, a pastor undergoes the heartache of watching the wayward turn his back on the Lord and return to old sinful habits. Additionally, there are times when a pastor longs to bring the church more in line with the Scriptures, but the congregation is not yet ready or willing to adopt the proposed changes.

If your husband's calling is in another sphere of life, perhaps he had to face an unpleasant boss, uncooperative employees, or was in some way unfairly treated. In our modern world employees often are required to maintain a frenetic pace at work in order to meet looming deadlines and keep ahead of the competition. In the midst of such a chaotic, stressful lifestyle we may ask with the hymn writer, 'Is this vile world a friend to grace to help me on to God?'

One of a wife's basic responsibilities is to provide a quiet, peaceful home for her husband, a refuge from outside cares and concerns. In a physical sense, this means a well-ordered, neat house. I know all about the challenge of trying to bring order out of chaos with energetic toddlers underfoot! However, resources are available to help us with this task. Visit your local library to find extremely practical books that helpfully explain how to complete daily household tasks ranging from general de-cluttering to keeping a kitchen sink sparkling. Organizational authors provide excellent pointers for those who feel so overwhelmed by the chaos that they have lost all hope of creating a well-ordered home. Seasons arrive in our lives when we can devote more time and energy to organizing the home, but sometimes the real problem may not be time or energy, but a plain lack of will power! 'Know yourself' is good advice, and do what you can to provide a harmonious, well-ordered home.

Related to this is establishing a disciplined routine. Do you have certain days set aside for specific domestic tasks? What time do you rise? When do you have that time in the day in which you can devote yourself personally to the Lord? Can your husband count on supper generally being ready at a certain time? When is bedtime? Creating habits like these will provide a structure for a quiet and peaceful life at home. Haphazard living and broken routines often lead to stress and anxiety.

Being a wife who is able to spend much time in training the children will help to provide a peaceful, quiet home for the husband. Mothers have a vital role to play in teaching and nurturing young ones in the ways of the Lord (see *1 Tim.* 1:5; *Prov.* 1:8, 9; *Titus* 2:4). If the children are living disciplined, happy lives and are learning to be self-controlled, the atmosphere in the family home will be peaceful. No father wants to return home every evening to be told by a weak and inattentive mother that the discipline of their unruly children is solely his task.

In a peaceful, quiet home the husband is protected to some degree from the outside world. Do not let the telephone unnecessarily break that peace. In the USA a simple way to alleviate the pressure from telemarketers is to add your number to the national do-not-call registry at www.donotcall.gov/. Similar services are available in other countries. Further, be the one who answers the phone and thereby screens his calls. If he finally has time to spend with the children and receives a phone call from the police association requesting donations for deserving youngsters to attend the circus, tell the caller that he is unavailable. This is just one example of how to protect your family time from outside intrusions.

My father often says 'Timing is everything.' The minute your husband walks in the door, having faced whatever challenges came his way in the ministry, is probably not the best time to unload all the cares of your heart to him. Give him some time to eat (!) and relax before adding to his burdens.

If your husband is a pastor, then, by providing a quiet, peaceful home you can help him fulfil his responsibility to show hospitality to others in need. When our houses are chaotic and disorganized it is difficult to invite others home. A quiet and peaceful home is a testimony to God's grace in a world filled with noise and strife.

We have looked at the need for a quiet, peaceful home, and at some of the ways to provide it. However, this will require work — *hard* work. It is largely a matter of priorities. You will need to *be there* to make a peaceful home for your husband. Houses do not magically turn into homes. I am not advocating that we all go back to college and major in interior design, or that we should learn cute crafts. Edith Schaeffer's wonderful book, *The Hidden Art of Homemaking*, describes simple ways to beautify our homes on a budget. She notes, 'This place should be expressing something of yourself. It should be communicating something of *you* to your visitors, but it should also satisfy something within you. You should *feel* "at home" here, because you have made it home with something of yourself.'[1]

If we want to provide a quiet, peaceful home for our husbands, we ourselves also need to be at peace. Ask yourself these important questions: Am I at peace with God? Do I know that my sins are forgiven through the death of Christ on the cross? Do I trust in him for salvation? Have I given up my will in submission to his? We are assured in Romans 5:1, 'Therefore, being justified by faith, we have peace with God through our Lord Jesus Christ.'

Further ask, am I experiencing the peace of God in my life or am I troubled about many things? Have I learned like Mary that the one thing needful is to sit at the feet of Jesus or am I more like Martha, agitated and worried about household duties? Am I at peace with God's providence in my life at this time? Concerning this subject Charles and Norma Ellis write: 'Is it fitting for a Christian wife, even a minister's wife, to complain about having to live in a certain city or area in which her husband's position has placed them? As helpers to our spouse we need to approach such a situation positively, and build a beautiful home life wherever we live geographically, being mindful that we, like Paul, can learn to be content "in whatsoever state" our Sovereign God has placed us.'[2]

[1] Edith Schaeffer, *The Hidden Art of Homemaking*, Wheaton, Illinois: Tyndale House Publishers, 1971, p. 66.

[2] Charles and Norma Ellis, *Heirs Together of Life* (Edinburgh: Banner of Truth, 1980), p. 251.

And finally, ask, Am I at peace with others? Do I have a complaining spirit, or am I gentle? Am I irritable with my husband or children? What kind of wife does my husband come home to? Am I seeking to adorn myself with 'the incorruptible beauty of a gentle and quiet spirit, which is very precious in the sight of God' (*1 Pet.* 3:4)? Our answers to these questions will be good indicators of the peacefulness of our homes.

> Drop Thy still dews of quietness,
> Till all our strivings cease;
> Take from our souls the strain and stress,
> And let our ordered lives confess
> The beauty of Thy peace.
>
> *John Greenleaf Whittier*

2

FULFIL YOUR RESPONSIBILITIES AS A MOTHER, BEFORE SEEKING OTHER MINISTRIES IN THE CHURCH

Behold, children are a heritage from the LORD, the fruit of
the womb is a reward (*Psa.* 127:3).

The wise Preacher reminds us that 'to everything there is a season, a time for every purpose under heaven' (*Eccles.* 3:1). That principle can be clearly observed in the natural world. In Pennsylvania, where I am writing this booklet, the beautiful autumn season has just begun. Yesterday, while driving across the state on the turnpike, I was delighted to see the lovely rolling hills and farmland that have been touched by colder temperatures and that are starting to change colour. What a pleasure to be in a climate that has four distinct seasons!

While we relish the variety of the seasons, we also recognize that with each season come specific responsibilities. In springtime we plant crops, in summer we mow the lawn, in autumn we rake the leaves, and in the winter we shovel snow. We would not think of harvesting apples and cooking apple-sauce in the springtime, nor would we plant carrot seeds in the autumn. Every season of the year has its corresponding tasks.

Similarly, life has its seasons. Each season knows its own particular joys and challenges. We must remember to rejoice in each season because 'this is the will of God in Christ Jesus for you' (*1 Thess.* 5:18). Our heavenly Father appoints our days, including our limitations and opportunities. While we should plan ahead, God sometimes overrides our plans for our good and his glory. During our time in Georgia, I spotted a wayside pulpit that proclaimed this thought in a striking way:

> Write your plans in pencil, but give God the eraser.

Jim Elliot, the martyred twentieth-century missionary to the Waodani tribe in Ecuador once wrote: 'Wherever you are, be all there. Live to the hilt every situation you believe to be the will of God.'[1] Why should we pine when we can enjoy contentment?

> Through all the changing scenes of life,
> In trouble and in joy,
> The praises of my God shall still
> My heart and tongue employ.

> *Psalm 34* in *A New Version of the Psalms of David*, 1698.

Not only must we learn to accept God's will in the changing seasons of life, but we must also accept the needful tasks which belong to those particular seasons. Before we were married we may have had more time to devote to personal interests and hobbies. Perhaps when we were 'foot loose and fancy free' we had more time to spend on ourselves and could choose how we wanted to be

[1] Quoted in Elisabeth Elliot, *Let Me Be a Woman*, (Wheaton: Tyndale House Publishers, 1976), p. 26.

occupied. But now that we are married, we must work together as a team and think how we can bring most benefit to the new family unit that God has created. Middle age brings with it new and increased responsibilities that were not present in our youth. We may need to care for ailing parents, or start a 'taxi service' for our children's sporting, musical, and social activities. Old age is a season of life that may require passing on the baton of leadership to the younger generation, or learning to cope with failing health. In whatever season of life we find ourselves, we must accept it as a gift from God's hand and seek to glorify him in our peculiar circumstances, cheerfully fulfilling the tasks belonging to our lot. In this chapter, we will specifically look at life's season of motherhood.

How often do you think about the privilege of motherhood? For it *is* a privilege to be used by God to mould the character of a little child, and to teach 'the lessons of our youth – honour, gratitude, and truth.' Every mother has received the high calling of training little ones for the Lord. Our children are lent to us by God so that we can 'bring them up in the training and admonition of the Lord' (*Eph.* 6:4). Walter J. Chantry, in his booklet, *The High Calling of Motherhood*, writes:

> It is a mother's task and privilege to oversee the forging of a personality in her sons and daughters. For this she must set a tone in the home which builds strong character. Hers it is to take great Christian principles and practically apply them in everyday affairs – doing it simply and naturally. It is her responsibility to analyse each child mentally, physically, socially, spiritually. Talents are to be developed, virtues must be instilled, faults are to be patiently corrected, young sinners are to be evangelized. She is building men and women for God. Results may not be visible until she has laboured for fifteen or twenty years. Even when her task ends, the true measure of her work awaits the full maturity of her children.[1]

[1] Walter J. Chantry, *The High Calling of Motherhood* (Edinburgh: Banner of Truth, 1986).

However, we live in a time when the virtues of motherhood are discounted and undervalued. So much attention in our culture is given to self-fulfilment, self-gratification, and self-actualization. Motherhood, on the other hand, is all about caring for the needs of another. It involves self-giving and self-denial. Elisabeth Elliot writes:

> Maturity starts with the willingness to give oneself. Childishness is characterized by self-centeredness. It is only the emotionally and spiritually mature who are able to lay down their lives for others, those who are 'masters of themselves that they might be the servants of others'.[1]

If we are going to fulfil our responsibilities as mothers to our children, we need to recognize that *time* is an important factor. Motherhood is a task the goals of which can only be achieved in the long-term; it is a marathon rather than a sprint. Motherhood will demand our time, and that is something we must recognize immediately. Other tasks have to be set aside for a season. Sometimes we may have to choose, not between the good and the bad, but between the good and the better, or best. While opportunities abound for women to serve the Lord by ministering to others outside the home and in the broader spheres of life, children must come first in a mother's list of priorities.

Little babies require considerable physical attention. They need to be fed, clothed, diapered, washed, held, comforted, and loved. They are so helpless physically and are totally dependent on our care. The needs of infants are constant and time-consuming. We have a choice: will we chafe under this demanding schedule or will we thank God for this season of motherhood he has given us?

When I was in the midst of rearing little ones at home, my aunt (who was a mother of four children), related to me that she had been glad to nurse her youngest baby in the middle of the night, because it gave her time alone with him that she did not have during the day when her other children were wide awake. What a good perspective! The choice was hers, Will I complain about the

[1] *Let Me Be a Woman*, p. 181.

intrusion on my time for rest, or will I find reason to rejoice? As children grow older they continue to need their mother to teach them. Mothers are stewards of these 'gifts from God', and we are responsible to lead our children to the Saviour. We need to tell them the stories of the Bible, instructing them in Bible doctrines that will help keep them from error and point them to faith in Christ. In his book, *Shepherding a Child's Heart*, Tedd Tripp maintains:

> Teaching your children to live for the glory of God must be your overarching objective. You must teach your children that for them, as for all mankind, life is found in knowing and serving the true and living God. The only worthy goal for life is to glorify God and enjoy Him forever.[1]

We desire to inculcate God-glorifying character traits in our children. We want them to turn from their natural sinful inclinations, and serve the Lord from an early age. Let us train our children to reverence God and his Word, to respect others, to be good mannered, to show gratitude to others, to be truthful in every relationship, to be humble and self-disciplined.

Again, to do this will take time and effort. A godly Scottish minister was visiting my parents' home when I was a young mother and recalled that often on Lord's Day afternoons when his daughter was a child, he would have preferred to take a nap, but instead spent the time teaching her lessons from the Word. She has now grown up and loves the Lord and how grateful is her father, who chose to spend his time doing something that has brought her lasting spiritual good.

This is a work that involves both great patience and careful instruction. In Isaiah's words, it will be 'line upon line, line upon line, here a little, there a little' (*Isa.* 28:10). Many lessons can be learned in the midst of daily life, as well as in a meticulously planned schedule of lessons. Flexibility with our time and a willingness to seize opportunities as they arise are very important to the successful

[1] Tedd Tripp, *Shepherding a Child's Heart* (Wapwallopen, Pennsylvania: Shepherd Press, 1995), pp. 76–7.

carrying out of this task. Deuteronomy 6:4 hints at the flexibility required of parents when it commands us to seize every available opportunity for instructing our children in the law of the Lord: Instruction can be given ' . . . when you sit in your house, when you walk by the way, when you lie down, and when you rise up'. The big question facing us as parents is: Are we willing to sacrifice our time and plans so that we are available for our children during those teachable seasons of their lives?

Mothers can occasionally feel that they are wasting their time staying at home with their children. Could we not be serving the Lord better in a larger, more public arena? Please do not despise the great opportunities for kingdom building in your own home! 'Raising a godly seed is still of the profoundest importance to the cause of God in the earth.'[1] A mother's work in training the next generation of Christ's church is vital and has far-reaching results. Timothy, a pastor in the early church, first learned the truths of the Bible from his mother Eunice and his grandmother Lois when just a very small boy: 'And that from childhood you have known the Holy Scriptures which are able to make you wise for salvation through faith which is in Christ Jesus' (2 Tim. 3:15). No task in the church or even on the mission field is of more importance for a mother than rearing her own children.

How are we going to fulfil this responsibility in the face of the apathy and opposition of the world? What if others in the church do not see the necessity of our mothering our children in this way? What will we do if others expect us to fulfil a ministry in the church that conflicts with our primary task as mothers? In the midst of opposition or misunderstanding from others, or even our own feelings of personal inadequacy, God's grace is sufficient for the task. He has promised that 'as your days, so shall your strength be' (Deut. 33:25). Be steadfast and persevere in sticking to your priorities. The Lord will help us and even use the peculiar challenges of motherhood for our own personal growth in grace.

[1] Chantry, The High Calling of Motherhood.

Father, I know that all my life
Is portioned out for me;
The changes that are sure to come,
I do not fear to see:
I ask Thee for a present mind,
Intent on pleasing Thee.

I would not have the restless will
That hurries to and fro,
Seeking for some great thing to do,
Or secret thing to know;
I would be treated as a child,
And guided where I go.

I ask Thee for the daily strength,
To none that ask denied,
A mind to blend with outward life,
While keeping at Thy side,
Content to fill a little space,
If Thou be glorified.

In service which Thy will appoints
There are no bonds for me;
My secret heart is taught the truth
That makes Thy children free;
A life of self-renouncing love
Is one of liberty.

Anna L. Waring

3

BE A SYMPATHETIC AND CONFIDENTIAL
LISTENER TO YOUR HUSBAND

Rejoice with those who rejoice, and weep with
those who weep (*Rom.* 12:15).

Few people in today's world know how to listen. Listening is an art which involves the mind, heart, and the whole body and not just the ears! It is important that we learn to be good listeners to our husbands.

A good listener is indeed a rare thing. Once while attending a ladies' retreat, I met a woman who was eager to tell me all about her family and background. As I listened to her story, I discovered some common ground between us.

However, when I began relating a little of my own situation, a blank expression came over her face and she made no comments by way of response to what I was saying. She clearly enjoyed talking about herself but did not show a corresponding joy in listening to what someone else wanted to say.

How can you become a good listener? The first requirement is to give your time and yourself to the other person. Be all there. If your husband needs to talk about a dilemma facing him, sit down, lay aside your other responsibilities for the moment, and give him your full attention.

You must also show him an understanding attitude. If someone, especially your husband, is going to open his heart to you, he is making himself vulnerable. Respect his openness with you and do not belittle or make light of the problem he is facing. Try to understand how large the matter looms in his eyes, and do not brush it aside as something insignificant.

Another way to show that you are listening to him is to repeat what he has told you in your own words. He will see that you were listening to him and that you also care about him. On the other hand, if you have misunderstood what he was telling you, then by repeating what you thought you heard him say allows for further clarification.

Body language is another important factor in being a good listener. Are you looking at your husband while he talks to you? Have you set aside your other tasks so that you can focus on what your husband is saying? Or are you rolling your eyes and sighing deeply as if you are bored and have your mind on something else? Think about what your expressions are revealing about you while you are listening to him. Is it boredom, irritation, impatience, or sarcasm? Or is it sympathy, concern, gentleness, and genuine interest?

It is helpful to try to put yourself in your husband's place as this will increase your sympathy for him. Inquire about background information, as appropriate, to be better able to appreciate the problem in its proper context.

Sometimes all you need to do is just listen. You might not be able to solve the problem, but the burden he shares will grow lighter for him because he knows you really do care for him. 'Bear one another's burdens, and so fulfil the law of Christ' (*Gal.* 6:2).

A word of caution is in order here. Have you ever noticed that we women like to pass on tidbits? This is fine when we are sharing delightful news of a recent conversion, a new baby, or a promotion at work. However, if the news is not edifying, then why are we sharing it? Your husband may have eased his burden by sharing it with you, but do you think he would be happy to know that you have shared his burden with others?

Keep your husband's confidence. One of the marks of the virtuous woman of Proverbs 31 is that she is trustworthy. Your husband needs to know that you will not only respect his vulnerability as he shares his concerns with you, but that you will keep these to yourself.

Wives, above all, make yourself available to your husbands. God's original declaration about man is as true today as it was in Eden:

'It is not good that man should be alone.' Christian wives, our husbands need us. Take up the responsibility, no, the privilege, of being your husband's companion and be available to listen to him.

My husband suggested I conclude this chapter by saying something that is sometimes forgotten or overlooked by pastors and churches. The pastor and his wife are not co-pastors. Pastors, the Lord called you and gave you the gifts for the ministry, not your wife. She does not need to know everything about church board meetings, counselling sessions, or proposed church policy. A church member once heard his pastor testify, 'I tell my wife everything; we're one flesh.' In that particular case some believed the well-informed wife to be in control of the church because of the way she controlled her husband.

Yes, feel free to seek your wife's advice on a particular matter, but do not burden her with more than she can or ought to carry. She may be a 'sounding board', not a 'board of elders'. She has not been called to lead the church; that is your calling and a responsibility you share with your fellow-elders.

> Oh! give Thine own sweet rest to me,
> That I may speak with soothing pow'r
> A word in season, as from Thee,
> To weary ones in needful hour.
>
> Oh! use me, Lord, use even me,
> Just as Thou wilt, and when, and where,
> Until Thy blessed face I see,
> Thy rest, Thy joy, Thy glory share.
>
> *Frances Ridley Havergal*

4

BE GENTLE IN ANALYSING YOUR HUSBAND'S SERMON FOR HIM!

She opens her mouth with wisdom, and on her tongue is the law of kindness (Prov. 31:26).

As we noted in a previous chapter, God created the woman to complete the man. It was not good for man to be alone and so God, in his wisdom and grace, provided the remedy for his loneliness. In like manner, God gave you to your husband to complete him. It was not good for your husband to be alone. Do you recognize your role of helping your husband? Do you realize that he needs you?

A wife stands in the closest relationship to her husband, closer than a parent to a child, or a brother to a brother. Peter refers to husband and wife being 'heirs together of the grace of life' (*1 Pet.* 3:7). I trust that you are your husband's best friend, and he yours. In marriage is found the deepest level of companionship, fellowship, and friendship that human beings experience. In this unique bond of fellowship, the husband will value his wife's opinions, or at least, he should!

When discussing your husband's sermon with him it is good to remember that Sunday evening can often be a discouraging time for a pastor. Timing is all important! Some years ago, a pastor's wife in the Midwest told me that on several occasions her husband felt like tendering his resignation on Monday mornings! By all accounts, his is not an isolated case. Perhaps a large number of church members were absent from the Lord's Day services, or a distraction hindered the full attention of the congregation to the sermon, or a visitor who at first seemed 'not far from the kingdom of God' left the service having lost all interest in the gospel. The parable of the sower shows us that God's enemy does all he can to snatch away the seed of the Word and keep it from taking root in the soil of the hearer's heart. The Bible also records how on several occasions some hearers believe while others mock the preacher's message.

Preaching is a mysterious and spiritual work. A man of God prepares a sermon, which may be doctrinally correct and full of timely exhortation or instruction, but without the Holy Spirit's blessing and power, the sermon will not produce the desired result. The words of the hymn are true, 'All is vain, unless the Spirit of the Holy One come down.' Preaching is not primarily about the man in the pulpit. Rather, it is the means that God uses to save sinners. Consequently, while one preacher may 'plant the seed' and another 'waters it', it is God who 'gives the increase'. Preachers look to God to bless their preaching with fruitful results in ways that motivational speakers or college lecturers do not.

During the preaching of a sermon pastors' wives must remember the exhortation to '…receive with meekness the implanted word' (*James* 1:21). We are part of the congregation and must listen to the voice of our Saviour in the spoken word. It is good for us to ask ourselves questions like: What has the Word of God taught me today? Has it pointed to a sin that I must confess? What promise has it encouraged me to claim? Is there a godly example for me to follow, a Christian grace to develop in my life? How should I apply the lessons of the sermon to my daily living? In other words, our goal should not be to critique our husbands' sermons, but to benefit spiritually from them.

In most cases following a sermon you do not need to state the obvious. Your husband knows very well if most of his congregation fell asleep during his sermon! He does not need you to inform him of that fact, or that you did not think he connected well with the people as he preached. Such comments can be like salt rubbed into a wound. However, if your husband tends to suffer from delusions about the quality of his preaching, then a word spoken in season may be required.

After the service your husband may ask for your opinion of his preaching. Before replying remember that God gave you to your husband to be his companion and suitable helper. Don't make fun of him. There is no room in a marriage for belittling one's spouse. State your opinion, but clothe your thoughts with generous, gracious and kind words. If, for instance, he mispronounced 'Chaldeans' or misquoted a verse during his sermon, gently correct him later, when you are alone together. Paul encourages us to speak 'the truth in love' (*Eph.* 4:15). Try to say something positive about the message. I'm sure you can think of something more substantial than, 'Your tie looked great!' Remember, our husbands do, or at least should, value our opinion and take to heart the loving wisdom we have to offer.

On other occasions you may want to raise a question to discuss together. Perhaps you disagreed with his analysis of the text or you might want to suggest another application from the passage. As your husband's best friend, you should be free to respectfully challenge his statements. Again, God gave you to your husband for a purpose and as 'iron sharpens iron, so a man sharpens the countenance of his friend' (*Prov.* 27:17). It is good for him to have someone who takes a real interest in his preaching work and with whom he can discuss its contents. Who knows but that the Lord may use you to keep your husband's feet on the solid ground of Scripture truth and keep him from falling into doctrinal error?

In all of our conversations with our husbands, we should not forget the peaks and troughs of the ministry. Faithfulness is the key. If one particular Sunday turned out to be a low point, urge your husband to persevere faithfully in the work of the ministry. After all, there will be another sermon to prepare for the next Lord's Day! Jesus' words of welcome into his eternal kingdom are not, 'Well done, good and successful servant'; rather, he will say, 'Well done, good and faithful servant' (*Matt.* 25:23). Paul reminds us that 'it is required in stewards that one be found faithful' (*1 Cor.* 4:2).

Our culture is fascinated by results and stories of spectacular success. The minister with the largest congregation, the most books in print, or the widest television ministry, is looked upon as being the most successful. Of course preachers want to give their all to the work of sowing and reaping, looking for the fruit of souls transformed by grace, but they must wait on the Lord of the harvest to give the increase. Even the great apostle Paul humbly confessed: 'I planted, Apollos watered, *but God gave the increase*' (*1 Cor.* 3:6).

5

ALWAYS SPEAK WELL OF YOUR HUSBAND IN PUBLIC

Let your speech always be with grace (*Col.* 4:6).

Endemic in our culture is an attitude of disrespect and self-centredness. Reverence for God and his Word and respect for other people are no longer common. Unfortunately even among Christians disrespectful attitudes sometime arise. A social gathering of Christian women does not give a green light to any of them to criticize their husbands. The apostle Paul concluded his statements about husbands and wives with the words, 'And let the wife see that she respects her husband' (*Eph.* 5:33).

What does it mean to respect your husband? It means to esteem him highly and treat him with love and honour. Respecting your husband in particular and other people in general, involves keeping the second great commandment, which is to 'love your neighbour as yourself' (*Matt.* 22:36-40). 1 Corinthians 13:4-7 expands our understanding of the character of this self-giving love, and the following verse, written by Susan H. Peterson, paraphrases those familiar words:

> Love is patient, kind, and selfless,
> Envies not, nor boasts in pride,
> Is not rude or quickly angered,
> Never holds a grudge inside.

Love does not delight in evil,
But with truth rejoices e'er;
Trusts, protects, and hopes forever,
Perseveres and always cares.

In addition to respecting him as a person made in the image of God, you should respect your husband for the God-given position he holds in your marriage. God created the institution of marriage and he so ordered it that the husband is the head of the home. Esteem your husband then as God's gift to you and a blessing for your life. The respect you have for your husband in your heart will show itself in your words and behaviour regarding him, both in his presence and in his absence. 'Out of the abundance of the heart the mouth speaks' (*Matt.* 12:34).

If you realize that God has commanded you to respect your husband and to treat him with love and honour, then you will be careful about how you speak about him to others. As a wife you will want to make your husband look good in the eyes of others. I remember attending a gathering of Christian women at a Christmas party and being disturbed by the disrespectful way some of the women were speaking about their husbands. Every foible and flaw was offered for public consumption! If I truly respect my husband I will want others to respect him too.

Positively, you could let others know your husband's strengths. For example, if there are areas in which your husband excels and for which he has won your deep appreciation, you could modestly mention these in the course of your conversation. In doing so you will be an encouragement to him. Generally speaking, we are not very good at speaking well of others. When was the last time you heard an enthusiastic comment about a third party? Edifying, uplifting, and encouraging words are rare commodities in a world that prefers sarcastic and salacious gossip.

Not every outwardly Christian marriage is God-centered. Evil invaded Eden's home, and to this day the family unit created by God faces attack from the enemy of souls.

Perhaps you are a Christian wife whose husband is living a double life; for you to respect your husband is not a simple or straightforward undertaking. What should you say and not say? And to whom should you say it? Well, if you do not have anything good to say about a person, then it is best to say nothing. A dear friend in a difficult marriage never once during our years of correspondence wrote a disrespectful word about her husband. Then again, she barely wrote a word about him at all. Her silence was an eloquent example of how to avoid being disrespectful.

If your husband is acting in a way that prevents you from having proper respect for him, try to talk with him about it. Please seek the help of a Christian friend or counsellor if the situation cannot be resolved between the two of you. However, the solution to your problem will never be found in tearing him down in public. Remember you are a team. God gave you to your husband to be a blessing to him, and one way you can bless him is to speak well of him in public.

6

BE COURTEOUS TO ALL MEMBERS OF THE CONGREGATION, SHOWING A CHRIST-LIKE SPIRIT TO ALL

And be kind to one another, tenderhearted, forgiving one another, even as God for Christ's sake has forgiven you (Eph. 4:32).

Many, if not all, of the responsibilities mentioned in this booklet are applicable to any Christian wife, but this particular responsibility is especially incumbent upon a pastor's wife. The pastor has the care of every member of the church. His call from the Chief Shepherd is to be an under-shepherd of God's flock in a local church setting. Though he may face opposition to his spiritual leadership in the church, he is to show kindness to all. The apostle Paul instructed Timothy that 'a servant of the Lord must not quarrel but be gentle to all, able to teach, patient, in humility correcting those who are in opposition, if God perhaps will grant them repentance, so that they may know the truth, and that they may come to their senses and escape the snare of the devil, having been taken captive by him to do his will' (2 Tim. 2:24–26). Peter addresses a similar situation when he teaches believers to have ' . . . your conduct honourable among the Gentiles, that when they speak against us as evildoers, they may, by our good works which they observe, glorify God in the day of visitation' (1 Pet. 2:12).

Sometimes opposition to the man of God will come from church members, or even church leaders. We are given a biblical example of this in the book of Acts when two godly missionaries, Paul and Barnabas, disagreed about taking John Mark along on their second missionary journey. 'Then the contention became so sharp that they parted from one another' (Acts 16:39). Reasonable men differ, and even in the body of Christ, godly men sometimes disagree.

How should we react when our husbands find themselves in the midst of opposition? If we are worth our salt we will want to stand by our husbands. Let your husband know that you are supporting him. Encourage him with your physical presence, if possible, when he faces some sort of opposition. If that is not possible, then assure him of your prayers as he enters the fray. Also, be available to listen when he returns from those times of conflict in the pastorate.

Whether the opposition comes from unbelievers, immature believers, or even church leaders, we must react in a way that is godly. Consider this exhortation of Paul to the believers at Colosse: 'Therefore, as the elect of God, holy and beloved, put on tender mercies, kindness, humility, meekness, longsuffering; bearing with one another, and forgiving one another, if anyone has a complaint against another; even as Christ forgave you, so you also must do' (Col. 3:12–13).

Early in our marriage, my husband presented a motion at a congregational business meeting. Fast and furious flew the arguments of other church members against his proposal. He decided not to pursue the motion in the face of such opposition. Later that night the tension in our home was so thick that you could have cut it with a knife. In fact, I went into labour about three hours after the meeting and gave birth the next day! I think the two events may have been connected.

With time, however, we learned that the vocal opponents had deeper concerns, which simply rose to the surface when my husband made his proposal. The opposition was not against him but against the direction they perceived the church was moving. The hostility you perceive may not be personal, so try to see the issue from the other person's perspective. Get past the badly chosen words and try to see the heart of the problem. This requires great patience, gentleness and, more often than not, a thick skin!

Sometimes our husbands can be on the receiving end of severe criticisms and rough treatment, but even then we are not to retaliate. On one occasion I accompanied my husband to a denominational meeting of pastors. A doctrinal disagreement had occurred and Scott was seeking reconciliation. Unfortunately, the olive branch he offered was not accepted and he was subjected to severe censures. Though grieved to hear these words, I was glad to be there by his side supporting him. But even such 'rough justice' does not permit responses in kind. 'Finally, . . . be tenderhearted, be courteous; not returning evil for evil or reviling for reviling, but on the contrary blessing, knowing that you were called to this, that you may inherit a blessing' (*1 Pet.* 3:8-9). Such occasions provide us with opportunities to evidence, by the grace of God, a humble, Christ-like spirit.

Thankfully, not all days in a pastor's life are filled with conflict and strife! It is a blessing from God to have church members who demonstrate support and appreciation for our husbands' labours in the ministry. To know that particular church members are praying daily for them is a tremendous encouragement.

Many who attend our services are teachable, eager students of God's Word, whose growth in grace gives great cause for the pastor to thank the Lord.

How should a pastor's wife befriend the members of her husband's church? Is it all right to have close friends? Is it all right to have one close friend? Can she ever let her hair down? Or must she seclude herself from everyone equally in order to create an aura of holy otherness because she is 'the pastor's wife'?

A pastor's wife must be friendly with all members of the church. I can remember how the pastor's wife in my home church was a great example of this very thing. She had such a splendid way of reaching out to each person, so that they all felt that she was a special friend. A pastor's wife should take an interest in members' concerns and joys. Learn about their families and pray for matters that come to your attention. Welcome them and receive them with a warm and genuine smile. Try to build others up by your encouraging comments. Send a sympathy note when members experience a loss. If possible, in the light of other responsibilities, join your husband on visits to the hospital or to the aged and infirm. If maternal responsibilities restrict such visits, make use of the telephone to brighten a widow's day or to let a troubled person in need know that you are praying for her. 'Rejoice with those who rejoice, and weep with those who weep' (*Rom.* 12:15).

> I ask Thee for a thoughtful love,
> Through constant watching wise,
> To meet the glad with joyful smiles,
> And to wipe the weeping eyes;
> And a heart at leisure from itself,
> To soothe and sympathize.
>   *Anna L. Waring*

It is impossible for any human being to have intimate friendships with scores of people. Accordingly, as pastors' wives, we cannot relate to every single church member at the same level. Because of similar life experiences, spiritual backgrounds, personalities, aptitudes, or interests, we will be drawn closer to some than to others. Be aware of this and don't spend all your time at public gatherings with your special friend or friends. This may involve denying yourself a level of closeness in the friendship that you know you would really enjoy. Perhaps a phone call from within the privacy of your own home might be a better way of pursuing deeper friendships.

I know some experienced voices advise that a pastor's wife ought not to develop friendships with other ladies from within the congregation. This is on account of the pastor being held in high esteem and the impropriety of allowing others to enter his inner circle. As in most areas of life, a balance is surely required, though it may be difficult to achieve. Be kind and pleasant to all, while unobtrusively enjoying closer friendships with a few. Be yourself, while keeping in mind that you represent your husband. Humbly avoid a superior, 'holier-than-thou', attitude; call to mind often that you are the Lord's.

Our responsibility to be kind and pleasant to all includes the children and teenagers of the church. Children need an affectionate word in season but are often overlooked by busy adults racing off to do something more important. Get acquainted with the children of your congregation and come down to their level, speaking to them with kindness. Display a genuine interest in their extra-curricular activities, academic endeavours, and spiritual concerns. Much good can be done by a simple word of encouragement or spiritual exhortation to young people.

Remember the other group often overlooked in churches – the strangers. In the Old Testament the Lord often commanded the children of Israel to be kind to the widow, the orphan, and the stranger. Such people lacked the blessings of family life, economic support, and social protection. God harbours a tender place in his heart for the stranger. We should be aware of the strangers who visit our churches and make a point of befriending them in a practical way. For instance, it will mean a lot to them to receive assistance in finding their way around the building, being introduced to others, or being invited home for a meal.

It is a sobering thought that others are watching our every move; more importantly, so is God! Keeping these things in mind will spur us on to honour him in our attitudes and actions towards all. We will need to show humility not only to the 'good and gentle, but also to the harsh' (*1 Pet.* 2:18). As pastors' wives we are called to be cheerful and friendly towards every member of our congregations. Sometimes our circumstances will require the grace of self-denial; but remember that every sacrifice we make is a thank-offering to the One who loved us and gave himself for us. And he knows what we give up for the benefit of others, and he cares for us too.

7

DON'T GOSSIP

Set a guard, O Lord, over my mouth; keep watch over
the door of my lips (*Psa.* 141:3).

A high school fellow student once took great delight in telling me about the three ways of communication: 'Telephone, telegram, and tell a woman'! It is hard to imagine two men spending hours on the telephone just chatting with each other. I have witnessed male telephone usage and have noticed to my amazement how it can sometimes terminate within just thirty seconds! Men get to the point, acquire the information they need, and move on with hardly a second thought. Of course there are exceptions, but most women would find such an exchange to be impolite, if not downright rude. We cushion our reason for making the call with polite questions about health, family, and recent activities. When we hear good news, we bubble over with excitement and need to share it with others right away. This can be good, when it is good news we are passing along.

The Christian faith we profess applies to all of life, not just to our actions, but also to our words, and even our inmost thoughts. Paul's exhortation to the Ephesians extends beyond mere words to the attitudes of the heart: 'Let all bitterness, wrath, anger, clamour, and evil speaking be put away from you, with all malice' (*Eph.* 4:31). In Romans 1:29 he includes whispering or gossiping in his catalogue of evil deeds. Therefore we need to be careful about what we say, but even more importantly, about what we think.

Some of the New Testament passages that address the subject of godliness in the life of women include the prohibition of slander or malicious gossip. In 1 Timothy we are given an outline of the qualifications required for church elders and deacons. These are accompanied by instructions concerning their wives: they are to 'be reverent, not slanderers' (*1 Tim.* 3:11). Paul also instructed Titus to exhort the older women to 'be reverent in behaviour, not slanderers' (*Titus* 2:3). Timothy was told that younger widows were not 'to be idle, wandering about from house to house . . . gossips and busybodies, saying things which they ought not' (*1 Tim.* 5:13).

The book of Proverbs, which is full of practical advice for daily living, warns against the sin of gossiping. 'A perverse man sows strife, and a whisperer separates the best of friends' (*Prov.* 16:28). 'A talebearer reveals secrets, but he who is of a faithful spirit conceals a matter (*Prov.* 11:13). 'Where there is no wood, the fire goes out; and where there is no talebearer, strife ceases' (*Prov.* 26:20).

So what is gossip? Based on the verses above, we can say that it is an evil thing in the eyes of God and something that harms other people. One dictionary defines it as 'idle talk, not always true, about other people and their affairs'.[1] Gossip is more likely to occur when we have too much free time on our hands, when we are careless with our speech, when we lack self-control over our words, or when we do not love our neighbour. It may include malice, the wishing of evil on a neighbour. It also usually takes place when the subject of the gossip is not present.

What is the solution to gossip? Scripture commands us to lay aside the evil works of our old, pre-converted selves and to put on the good works of our new selves in Christ. The Holy Spirit's life and work within us will be seen by other people in our Christ-like attitudes, words, and actions. In 1 Timothy 5 Paul speaks about the contrasting lifestyles of younger and older widows. The younger

[1] 'Gossip', *The World Book Dictionary*, (Chicago: Doubleday & Co., 1977), p. 919.

widows wandered idly from house to house and gossiped as they went. In contrast to them, the older widows were full of good works; these included bringing up children, giving hospitality to strangers, washing the disciples' feet, relieving the afflicted, and performing every good work (*1 Tim.* 5:10). Moreover, the younger widows who had all this time on their hands are exhorted to 'marry, bear children, manage the house, give no opportunity to the adversary to speak reproachfully' (*1 Tim.* 5:14). It seems then that one way to avoid the sin of gossiping is to keep busy at home!

My daughter's schoolteacher hung up a sign in the classroom to discourage the children from developing this evil habit. On the sign were three simple questions: 'Is it true? Is it kind? Is it necessary?' If we could only fix those questions clearly in our minds they would prevent unwelcome words from tumbling out of our mouths. How much trouble would they save us and others! We need to think before putting our mouths in gear.

Obviously, 'Is it true?' needs to be asked first of all. 'The ninth commandment forbids anything that gets in the way of the truth or injures anyone's reputation.'[1] Concerning the ninth commandment Starr Meade writes:

> We protect the reputations of others by being careful of what we say about them. We are also to protect others' reputations by being careful of what we *hear* about them . . . The bad things we hear about others stay with us and influence what we think of them. Even when we are not sure whether what we have heard is true, it stays in our minds and affects how we think of that person.[2]

The New Testament repeats the Old Testament command against falsehood when it says, 'Do not lie to one another, since you have

[1] *The Westminster Shorter Catechism in Modern English*, Reformed Theological Seminary, Jackson, Mississippi, 1986, as quoted in Starr Meade, *Training Hearts, Teaching Minds: Family Devotions Based on the Shorter Catechism* (Phillipsburg, New Jersey: Presbyterian & Reformed Publishing Company, 2000), p. 256.

[11] Meade, *Training Hearts*, p. 254.

put off the old man with his deeds, and have put on the new man ... ' (*Col.* 3:9, 10). If we are not sure that the tidbit is true, we must not repeat it to others.

The second question should prevent us from passing on certain facts that, while truthful, would nevertheless be unkind to repeat. Again, Paul tells us to put off certain types of destructive speech and replace them with contrasting Christian graces: 'And be kind to one another, tenderhearted, forgiving one another, even as God in Christ forgave you' (*Eph.* 4:32). It is recorded of the virtuous woman of Proverbs 31 that 'on her tongue is the law of kindness' (*Prov.* 31:26). Our words about others are to be loving and kind, never mean and vicious.

The third question will also temper the words we speak about another person. Does the person I am addressing really need to hear this piece of information about a third party? If it is not necessary, then I had better talk about something else altogether. Paul admonishes the believers in Ephesus when he says, 'Let no corrupt word proceed out of your mouth, but what is good for necessary edification, that it may impart grace to the hearers' (*Eph.* 4:29). Edification is all about building others up, not tearing them down. That verse emphasizes our need to consider carefully how our words will affect our listeners. Our words should be pure, good, necessary, edifying, and grace-giving. What a high standard the Bible sets for the Christian's speech!

As we saw earlier from Matthew 12:34, our speech is the evidence of what lies in our hearts. In order to purify the mouth the heart must be put right first. This is one of the reasons why Paul directs the Philippians to be careful of their thoughts: 'Finally, brethren, whatever things are true, whatever things are noble, whatever things are just, whatever things are pure, whatever things are lovely, whatever things are of good report, if there is any virtue and if there is anything praiseworthy – meditate on these things' (*Phil.* 4:8).

Proverbs 31:10–31 paints that wonderful picture of the virtuous woman. One of the characteristics of this godly woman is found in verse 11: 'The heart of her husband safely trusts her.' Does your husband trust you? Can he leave his concerns with you for safe keeping or does he have reason to doubt your ability to keep his confidence? At times a husband may share information with his wife that is not public knowledge, items of a delicate nature that need to be handled cautiously and wisely. Perhaps he needs to unburden his heart to you or may simply want your wise opinion. At other times, he may request that you be present during an interview with a female parishioner. Your husband should feel comfortable in sharing confidential matters or the burdens of his heart with you. In other words, he should not fear that you will 'spill the beans' and pass on personal information to third parties. Keep such knowledge in the utmost confidence. A talkative woman can do terrible harm to both individuals and churches.

Now in whom does a pastor's wife confide when she needs to unburden her heart? Some time ago, a friend of mine belonged to a church in which the pastor's wife developed a friendship with her. Some of the things the pastor's wife revealed about her husband caused my friend to lose respect for him and his ministry. It is there-fore perhaps better to find a 'bosom friend' from outside the ranks of your local church. If you have grave concerns about your marriage, seek help, but from a godly person outside the congreg-ation.

In short, we should only want to build others up with our speech. Let us humbly think the best about people and pass on the good news of God's grace at work in their lives. What good can we do by pointing to the flaws, inconsistencies, or sins of others? The golden rule applies to our speech: 'Therefore, whatever you want men to do to you, do also to them' (*Matt.* 7:12). If we make an honest, sober assessment of ourselves we will become very reluctant to gossip maliciously about others. Would we want our shortcomings to be discussed by other people? And finally, let us avoid idle chatter by diligently following our callings and busying ourselves with those good works that will glorify our Father in heaven.

8

FREELY DISAGREE IN PRIVATE ABOUT CHURCH POLICY WITH YOUR HUSBAND, BUT BE TIGHT-LIPPED WITH OTHER CHURCH MEMBERS

To everything there is a season, a time for every purpose
under heaven . . . a time to keep silence, and a time
to speak (*Eccles.* 3:1, 7).

So many of our responsibilities as pastors' wives relate to words. We need to be confidential listeners to our husbands, careful not to gossip, encourage others by gracious words, speak well of our husbands in public, and address others with kindness and love.

If you were not aware of it before you were married, then you soon realized after your wedding that you and your husband are different from one another! The differences may be many and varied. God gave you to your husband as a 'helper comparable to him' (*Gen.* 2:20). Your distinctive roles as husband and wife are complementary. What one lacks the other can provide and *vice versa*. We recognize and rejoice in our God-given physical differences. Indeed, we are two distinct individuals who bring our own peculiar perspectives to the marriage. We are not to be clones in our thinking. Our discernment can benefit our husbands when they need to make decisions. God gave you to your husband to be a blessing to him, so do not be shy about sharing your thoughts with him.

Sometimes we may find ourselves holding conflicting views about a certain matter of church policy or practice. How are we to address such an issue? Feel free to express your concerns privately to your husband; you may well find that your frankness with him may help him to see the issue more clearly. On the other hand, there may be more to the problem than you at first realized, and you may be the one who gets to see the matter more clearly! Timing is the all-important factor here. It is best to raise such things when you are alone together.

In the course of interacting with church members you may find that some of them may also disagree with the church's position on certain matters and may want to discuss them with you. I can remember an occasion when I came to a different position from the church on a particular issue. I was convinced of the rightness of my position, having studied the Scriptures and consulted a few commentaries! I talked things over with my husband, but did so in private, behind closed doors. However, one day when visiting a widow in the congregation, I discovered that she too held a perspective on this issue similar to my own. It was so tempting to share my point of view and to discuss the matter openly with her. However, I decided it would be best to keep silent and not to express my support for her viewpoint. This was not an easy thing to do, but the need for exercising the grace of self-denial was obvious. Yes, sometimes we may have to give up expressing our own opinions for the greater good of the body of Christ.

Perhaps this is straying from the point a little, but sometimes a loving pastor has to be patient with his congregation because they do not share his understanding of Scripture on a certain subject, or may not yet be ready to make the changes he would like to see. I am not referring here to sinful practices that directly contradict the Word of God, but to other things in a church that may be permitted to continue until the congregation receives more light on the subject and is willing to make the necessary changes.

What a fine line a pastor must sometimes walk when attempting to reform a church according to the Word of God! Good work in churches has come to nothing, all because a domineering pastor has ridden roughshod over a congregation, making demands for sweeping changes of which his people are not yet convinced. The work of reforming a church is more often a marathon than a sprint; lasting fruit is produced through great patience and careful instruction (cf. *2 Tim.* 4:2).

In conclusion, remember that you and your husband are yoked together in marriage. In the family unit you should always side with each other in front of the children. When you differ with your husband about family matters, keep your discussions private. Your children need to be assured that Mom and Dad will always stick together and will back each other up. The united front you display in the home should also be evident in the church. Do not lead those who are agitating for a change in some church policy. Rather, support your husband. Remember, you are a team!

> If I have wounded any soul today,
> If I have caused one foot to go astray today,
> If I have walked in my own wilful way,
> Dear Lord, forgive!
>
> If I have uttered idle words or vain,
> If I have turned aside from want or pain,
> Lest I myself should suffer through the strain,
> Dear Lord, forgive!
>
> Forgive the sins I have confessed to Thee,
> Forgive the secret sins I do not see;
> O guide me, love me, and my keeper be,
> Dear Lord, Amen.
>
> *C. Maude Battersby*

9

THROUGH ENCOURAGEMENT AND PRAYER, BE YOUR HUSBAND'S CHIEF SUPPORTER

Be of good courage, and he shall strengthen your heart,
all you who hope in the LORD (*Psa.* 31:24).

'My work is to keep him in the pulpit' (Bethan Lloyd-Jones,
speaking of her husband, Dr Martyn Lloyd-Jones).[1]

T he ministry can be a lonely, discouraging place, and all of us as
church members should strive to support our pastors with lots
of encouragement. The Bible commands us to support our ministers: 'Let him who is taught the word share in all good things with
him who teaches' (*Gal.* 6:6). Paul's words to the Galatians specifically refer to the provision of the pastor's material needs. It is our
responsibility to give money for their financial support. Paul also
exhorts the believers in Thessalonica 'to recognize those who labour
among you, and are over you in the Lord and admonish you, and to
esteem them very highly in love for their work's sake. Be at peace
among yourselves' (*1 Thess.* 5:12–13). The author of the letter to the
Hebrews gives a similar instruction: 'Remember those who rule over
you, who have spoken the word of God to you, whose faith follow,
considering the outcome of their conduct' (*Heb.* 13:7). How many
problems in the ministry would be solved if church members memor-
ized such verses and daily put them into practice!

Particular difficulties attend the work of the minister. Lack of
visible fruit can be a profound source of discouragement. A scant
interest on the part of his hearers can dampen the spirits of the most

[1] Quoted in Murray, *D. Martyn Lloyd-Jones: The Fight of Faith*, p. 761.

fervent preacher. He can bear well the opposition of the world to the gospel message, but how can one bear to see brother against brother within the fellowship of the church? The times in which we live can also weigh heavily upon the heart of the man of God. Evil abounds on every side and seems to increase daily in strength. The times of longed for revival and refreshing from the Lord have not yet appeared. So many Christian folk are consumed with 'the cares of this world, the deceitfulness of riches, and the desires for other things' (*Mark* 4:19).

> The things of earth have fill'd our thought,
> And trifles of the passing hour.
>
> *Thomas Benson Pollock*

Thomas Kelly must have known something of the discouragements inherent in the ministry when he penned the following verses in his hymn, 'Speed Thy Servants':

> Where no fruit appears to cheer them,
> And they seem to toil in vain,
> Then in mercy, Lord, draw near them,
> Then their sinking hopes sustain:
> Thus supported,
> Let their zeal revive again.
>
> In the midst of opposition
> Let them trust, O Lord, in Thee;
> When success attends their mission,
> Let Thy servants humbler be:
> Never leave them
> Till Thy face in heav'n they see.

J. C. Ryle, commenting on John 4:31–42, wrote:

Work for the souls of men, is undoubtedly attended by great discouragements. The heart of natural man is very hard and unbelieving. The blindness of most men to their own lost condition and peril of ruin is something past description . . . No one can have any conception of the small number of those who repent and believe, until he has personally endeavoured to 'save some' . . .

The true antidote against despondency in God's work is an abiding recollection of such promises as that before us. There are 'wages' laid up for faithful reapers. They shall receive a reward at the last day, far exceeding anything they have done for Christ, — a reward proportioned not to their success, but to the quantity of their work. They are gathering 'fruit', which shall endure when this world has passed away, — fruit, in some souls saved, if many will not believe, and fruit in evidences of their own faithfulness, to be brought out before assembled worlds. Do our hands ever hang down, and our knees wax faint? Do we feel disposed to say, 'My labour is in vain and my words without profit'? Let us lean back at such seasons on this glorious promise. There are 'wages' yet to be paid. There is 'fruit' yet to be exhibited. . . . Let us work on. One single soul saved, shall outlive and outweigh all the kingdoms of the world.[1]

Perhaps your husband is occupied in another calling. Discouragement is by no means limited to the pastoral office! Men can experience great disappointment in their various callings by discovering that their well-laid plans have come to nothing. This may happen after years of faithful labour. Perhaps the discouragement comes from God's providential dealings in their lives, from others' opposition, or from feelings of personal inadequacy.

What should our response be if our husbands are despondent in their work? Don't be like Job's wife who, after Job had suffered the loss of children, wealth, and health, told him to 'Curse God, and die'! (*Job* 2:9). Looking at the outward circumstances she became disheartened and embittered and spoke discouragingly to her husband.

[1] J. C. Ryle, *Expository Thoughts on the Gospels – John,* vol. 1, (1869; repr. Edinburgh: Banner of Truth, 1987), pp. 240–1.

However, Jonathan, the son of King Saul, provides us with a better example. David was hiding in the mountains of the Wilderness of Ziph because King Saul daily tried to kill him. In the midst of his desperate struggle for survival, 'Jonathan, Saul's son, arose and went to David in the woods and strengthened his hand in God. And he said to him, "Do not fear, for the hand of Saul my father shall not find you. You shall be king over Israel, and I shall be next to you. Even my father Saul knows that"' (*1 Sam.* 23:16, 17). Jonathan observed that David was wrestling with discouragement. The royal prince was a thoughtful person who looked upon his circumstances with a spiritual mind. He encouraged David in his God. Had the Lord not promised David the throne of Israel? 'David, remember God's unchangeable and unbreakable word to you.'

In the same way we must use our skills of observation. What are the clues that your husband is discouraged? Learn to read him, so that you will know how best to help him. Wives can greatly help their husbands overcome discouragement. 'Men are observed often to become easily discouraged, but to women has been given the gift of a faith or optimism or vision which enables them to provide encouragement in time of need.'[1] Ultimately God is the source of the encouragement we give to our husbands. The promises of God are our rock and hope. Learn them, memorize them, and be ready to encourage your husband with them. The Psalms in particular offer many encouragements for us to trust in God.

How do we respond to discouragement? Are we particularly prone to be discouraged? Do we drag our husbands down or do we lift up their spirits? Let us make it our aim to emulate the righteous man, should we, like him, receive disheartening news: 'He will not be afraid of evil tidings; his heart is steadfast, trusting in the LORD' (*Psa.* 112:7). Stay close to the Lord so that when trouble does strike, you will respond like Jonathan, and not like Job's wife.

You probably know your husband better than anyone else in the world. Use your knowledge to pray intelligently for him. 'Is anyone

[1] Charles and Norma Ellis, *Heirs Together*, pp. 64–5.

among you suffering? Let him pray' (*James* 5:13). If you know his particular weaknesses or struggles against remaining sin, pray! If you know that he is disheartened with regard to some aspect of his calling, pray! If you are concerned about a character flaw in his life, pray! And let him know that you are praying for him. That knowledge in itself can be a wonderful support to him.

If you are not sure how to pray for your husband, then try using the prayers of Paul found in his epistles; fill in your husband's name in the prayer. Colossians 1:9–11 is a good example, and this is how I would use this prayer to intercede for my husband:

> For this reason I also pray for Scott, and . . . ask that he may be filled with the knowledge of God's will in all wisdom and spiritual understanding; that he may walk worthy of the Lord, fully pleasing him, being fruitful in every good work and increasing in the knowledge of God; strengthened with all might, according to his glorious power, for all patience and longsuffering with joy . . . '

Additionally, we can also make use of the prayer requests that Paul shared with his friends. For instance, in Ephesians 6:19–20 he writes, '[praying] for me, that utterance may be given to me, that I may open my mouth boldly to make known the mystery of the gospel, for which I am an ambassador in chains; that in it I may speak boldly, as I ought to speak.' Greater responsibility rests on those who are shepherds of God's flock (see *Ezek.* 34; *James* 3:1). Therefore, our prayers should include requests for preservation from error in doctrine and protection from sin. More is at stake than the pastor's individual standing before God, for if he turns away from the true faith to doctrinal error or begins to practise a sinful lifestyle, then the people of God under his care may be led astray too.

God gave man a good gift in marriage. Our Reformed confessions of faith list three particular benefits from the marriage covenant: companionship, the avoidance of immorality, and the blessing of children. As wives we want to give ourselves to our husbands so that they will always be 'enraptured' by our love (cf. *Prov.* 5:1–23, especially 18–19). Our decadent Western culture is permeated with temptations to sexual sin. Pastors are particularly susceptible to this temptation and must be on their guard in their dealings with women in the course of their ministry. Many are the sad stories that could be related of men whose lives and ministries have been ruined by an unguarded moment. Moreover, the Internet has made pornography much more easily available and accessible. Be aware of your husband's activities and hold him accountable. John R. Sittema writes, An 'elder will be wise never to visit a single woman alone. Not only must he be aware of the potential damage to reputations (both hers and his) of wagging tongues, but he must also be aware of the danger of temptation to his and her flesh. No elder is beyond such temptation himself; any who thinks he is, is either naïve or spiritually arrogant.'[1] In addressing the subject of how to avoid sexual immorality, Paul in 1 Corinthians 7:1–5 encourages the wife and the husband to give each other their conjugal rights and not to withhold them, 'except with consent for a time, that you may give yourselves to fasting and prayer'; but then he adds, 'and come together again so that Satan does not tempt you because of your lack of self-control.'

In our prayers for those of our husbands who are also pastors we must remember the spiritual aspect of the preaching ministry. While we pray for clarity of thought and speech for them, we must also earnestly pray that the power of the Holy Spirit will attend their preaching. One of our hymns expresses this dependence on the Lord:

> Bless Thy Word that it may prove
> Rich in fruits that Thou dost love.

The work of the sermon doesn't stop at noon; may the Lord make the implanted word grow in the hearts of all who heard it.

We may need to encourage our pastor-husbands to continue steadfast in their calling. So many voices today call for the pastor to fulfil a plethora of duties aside from the primary tasks of prayer and

[1] John R. Sittema, *With a Shepherd's Heart: Reclaiming the Pastoral Office of Elder* (Grandville, Michigan: Reformed Fellowship, Inc., 1996).

preaching. But what is the purpose of the ministry? Paul exhorted Timothy:

> Preach the word! Be ready in season and out of season. Convince, rebuke, exhort, with all longsuffering and teaching. For the time will come when they will not endure sound doctrine, but according to their own desires, because they have itching ears, they will heap up for themselves teachers; and they will turn their ears away from the truth, and be turned aside to fables' (*2 Tim.* 4:2–4).

In the face of today's widespread aversion to expository preaching, we must encourage our husbands to stick to the God-ordained means of salvation, 'the message preached' (*1 Cor.* 1:21).

Sometimes our husbands may need a word of rebuke to get them out of a despondent mood. When Job's wife told him to curse God and die, he rebuked her for such a discouraging word: 'But he said to her, "You speak as one of the foolish women speaks. Shall we indeed accept good from God, and shall we not accept adversity?"' (*Job* 2:10). If we can keep our eyes focused on our sovereign God who works all things according to his will, then we can help our husbands to rise above the outward, visible, temporary circumstances that confront them. Like Paul 'we do not lose heart . . . while we do not look at the things which are seen, but at the things which are not seen. For the things which are seen are temporary, but the things which are not seen are eternal' (*2 Cor.* 4:18).

> Turn your eyes upon Jesus,
> Look full in His wonderful face,
> And the things of earth will grow strangely dim,
> In the light of His glory and grace.
>
> *Helen Lemmel*

We have thought in this chapter about encouraging our husbands by directing them to the Lord and the promises of his Word, to eternal realities rather than temporal circumstances, and by praying for them. Perhaps your wedding vows, like mine, included the promise to be your husband's 'faithful, loving, and encouraging wife'. Very practically speaking, what are some of the ways in which we can fulfil the role of an encourager? Besides surprising him with a little note or a phone call, have you ever thought about creating something like an 'encouragement file' for your husband? If you should come across a particular Bible verse that you believe is very appropriate for him in his situation, jot it down and tuck it into this folder. Perhaps you have found a quote from a Christian author that you know would raise his sinking spirits; that also could go into the folder. The great hymns of the faith, many of which were written out of the crucible of suffering, can lift up our thoughts to our great God and provide wonderful thoughts for meditation in our discouraging moments. Why not suggest to your husband that he also uses this folder to keep a record of the occasional notes written by members of the congregation in appreciation for his ministry? All these are tokens of God's goodness and grace, upon which he can reflect, as and when occasion demands.

10

REMEMBER THAT YOUR HUSBAND IS JUDGED IN PART BY YOUR BEHAVIOUR – BE AN ASSET, NOT A LIABILITY, TO HIM

Only let your conduct be worthy of the gospel
of Christ (*Phil.* 1:27).

Marriage is a bond that unites a man and a woman together for life. No longer can the individual consider only himself when making decisions. The family unit of husband and wife is now of primary importance. The married couple has a common identity and purpose. A wife's actions and speech will reflect on her husband. For better or worse her reputation is tied to her husband's and his to hers.

While it is true that every wife may adorn or mar her husband's reputation, the pastor's wife especially must realize the importance of living a life of holiness. The pastor's family can disqualify him from the ministry. In 1 Timothy 3, among the qualifications Paul lists for elders and deacons is an exemplary home: the elder is to 'rule his own house well, having his children in submission with all reverence (for if a man does not know how to rule his own house, how will he take care of the church of God?)' (*1 Tim.* 3:4–5). Moreover, the wives of church leaders must be 'reverent, not slanderers, temperate, faithful in all things' (*1 Tim.* 3:11).

In the Scriptures there is a strong connection between sound doctrine and godly living. Titus is commanded to 'speak the things which are proper for sound doctrine' (*Titus* 2:1). Later in the same chapter Paul tells him that bondservants are to live in a godly manner so 'that they may adorn the doctrine of God our Saviour in all things'. To be a Christian is much, much more than merely saying you believe in an orthodox creed; it is a life that is being transformed by the truth we believe.

In particular, the Scriptures call upon Christian women to be submissive to their own husbands (*1 Pet.* 3:1) and chaste in their conduct (*1 Pet.* 3:2), to adorn themselves with the incorruptible beauty of a gentle and quiet spirit (*1 Pet.* 3:4), to trust in God (*1 Pet.* 3:5), to be reverent in their behaviour, not to slander, not to give themselves to much wine, to be teachers of good things, to be loving toward their husbands and children, to be discreet, to be homemakers, to be good (*Titus* 2:3–5), to be well reported for their good works (*1 Tim.* 5:10), to be hospitable to the needy, self-controlled, faithful (*1 Tim.* 3:11), and modest (*1 Tim.* 2:9).

For the sake of the gospel we must exercise great care not to give others any reason to think ill of our husbands. Whether we like it or not, our actions reflect on them. We may need to exercise the grace of self-denial. Perhaps our husbands are serving among untaught or young and immature believers. There may be areas of conduct that we will choose to avoid because of the 'weaker brother' principle. Remember how Paul declared: 'We give no offence in anything, that our ministry may not be blamed' (*2 Cor.* 6:3). We may need to think through areas of Christian liberty for the sake of the gospel and be willing to give up our right to do something, lest we harm Christians who are weak in the faith. This is why Paul says to the Romans: 'We then who are strong ought to bear with the scruples of the weak, and not to please ourselves. Let each of us please his neighbour for his good, leading to edification' (*Rom.* 15:1–2).

Again, whether we like it or not, if you are a pastor's wife, you are an example. Your husband is called to be an example to the flock of God (*1 Pet.* 5:3) and because you are one with him, you are a part of his example. Perhaps you did not enter into marriage knowing that your husband would be called to the ministry. This was true for me: I married an aeronautical engineer who became a pastor ten years later. But we believe this is where God has placed us and it is good to cheerfully accept God's providences in becoming a pastor's wife.

> Only be still, and wait His leisure
> In cheerful hope, with heart content
> To take whate'er thy Father's pleasure
> And all-discerning love hath sent;
> Nor doubt our inmost wants are known
> To Him who chose us for His own.
>
> *Georg Neumark*

When you become aware that you are an example to others, you will be especially careful to keep a watch on your words, your behaviour, and your children. The reason we want to be a good example to others is that we might adorn the doctrine of God in all things so that others will want to follow our Lord and Saviour.

Above all, be like Christ: 'Be holy for I am holy' (*1 Pet.* 1:16). Though we greatly desire to honour our husbands by our lifestyle, our greatest concern is to bring honour to our Saviour. What should grieve our hearts most of all is the thought of dishonouring the name of Christ. The reason given in Titus 2:5 for godly behaviour in young women is 'that the word of God may not be blasphemed'. Likewise, the reason given in 1 Timothy 5:14 for younger women to be homemakers and care for their families is to 'give no opportunity to the adversary to speak reproachfully'.

May the Lord help each of us to live holy lives so that we will become a crown to our husbands and so that the name of our great God will be honoured.

> Take time to be holy,
> Speak oft with thy Lord;
> Abide in Him always,
> And feed on His Word.
> Make friends of God's children;
> Help those who are weak;
> Forgetting in nothing
> His blessing to seek.
>
> Take time to be holy,
> The world rushes on;
> Spend much time in secret
> With Jesus alone.
> By looking to Jesus,
> Like Him thou shalt be;
> Thy friends in thy conduct
> His likeness shall see.
>
> *William D. Longstaff*

CONCLUSION

When pondering our Christian responsibilities it is easy to become overwhelmed by the sheer size of the task facing us. However, it is the Lord who has given us to our husbands and his grace will enable us to be the Christian wives he calls us to be. God's grace shines brightest in the lives of those who are most conscious of their weakness and failures. How amazing it is that the man who considered himself 'the least of the apostles', 'less than the least of all the saints', and even 'the chief of sinners' was also one of God's 'fellow workers' (*1 Cor.* 3:9)! He knew strength in weakness and found God's grace more than sufficient for all his needs. You too will experience that same grace as you labour on with 'joy to do the Father's will'. May God's richest blessings be upon all faithful wives who minister to the minister or who support their husbands in their respective callings. 'But you, be strong and do not let your hand be weak, for your work shall be rewarded!' (*2 Chron.* 14:7).

Finally, let us conclude our thoughts with Isaac Watts' heartfelt prayer for God's glory to be revealed increasingly on the earth through the church:

> Pity the nations, O our God!
> Constrain the earth to come,
> Send Thy victorious Word abroad;
> And bring the strangers home.
>
> We long to see Thy churches full,
> That all the chosen race
> May, with one voice and heart and soul,
> Sing Thy redeeming grace.

Bibliography

WALTER J. CHANTRY, *The High Calling of Motherhood* (Edinburgh: Banner of Truth, 1986).

ELISABETH ELLIOT, *Let Me Be a Woman* (Wheaton, Illinois: Tyndale House, 1976).

CHARLES & NORMA ELLIS, *Heirs Together of Life* (Edinburgh: Banner of Truth, 1980).

STARR MEADE, *Training Hearts, Teaching Minds: Family Devotions Based on the Shorter Catechism* (Phillipsburg, New Jersey: Presbyterian and Reformed, 2000).

IAIN H. MURRAY, *D. Martyn Lloyd-Jones: The Fight of Faith* (Edinburgh: Banner of Truth, 1990).

TEDD TRIPP, *Shepherding a Child's Heart* (Wapwallopen, Pennsylvania: Shepherd Press, 1995).

J. C. RYLE, *Expository Thoughts on the Gospels, John, vol. 1* (1869; Edinburgh: Banner of Truth, 1987).

EDITH SCHAEFFER, *The Hidden Art of Homemaking* (Wheaton, Illinois: Tyndale House Publishers, 1971).

The Westminster Shorter Catechism in Modern English (Jackson, Mississippi: Reformed Theological Seminary, 1986).

The World Book Dictionary (Chicago: Doubleday & Co., 1979).